Picture the Past
SHOPS

Jane Shuter

Heinemann
LIBRARY

First published in Great Britain by Heinemann Library
Halley Court, Jordan Hill, Oxford OX2 8EJ
a division of Reed Educational & Professional Publishing Ltd

OXFORD FLORENCE PRAGUE MADRID ATHENS
MELBOURNE AUCKLAND KUALA LUMPUR SINGAPORE TOKYO
IBADAN NAIROBI KAMPALA JOHANNESBURG GABORONE
PORTSMOUTH NH (USA) CHICAGO MEXICO CITY SAO PAULO

Designed by Ken Vail Graphic Design, Cambridge
Colour separations by Dot Gradations, Wickford, Essex
Printed in Malaysia by Times Offset (M) Sdn. Bhd.

01 00 99 98 97
10 9 8 7 6 5 4 3 2 1

ISBN 0 431 04258 6

British Library Cataloguing in Publication Data

Shuter, Jane
 Shops. – (Picture the past)
 1. Stores, Retail – History – Juvenile literature
 2. Stores, Retail– Pictorial works – Juvenile literature
 I. Title
 381.1'09

Acknowledgements
The authors and publishers would like to thank the following for permission to use
photographs and other illustrative material:
Beck Isle Museum, page 4 top;
The Peter Gillies Collection, page 4 bottom;
Hulton Getty, page 5;
Topham Picturepoint, pages 6, 8, 10, 12, 16, 18;
Oxfordshire Photographic Archive, pages 14, 20.

Cover photographs reproduced with permission of The Peter Gillies Collection,
Topham Picturepoint and Oxfordshire Photographic Archive.

Our thanks to Betty Root for her comments in the preparation of this book.

Every effort has been made to contact copyright holders of any material reproduced
in this book. Any omissions will be rectified in subsequent printings if notice is
given to the Publisher.

Contents

Some words are shown in bold text, **like this**. You can find out what these words mean by looking in the glossary on page 24.

Taking photos

People started taking photos in the 1830s. It took over an hour to take a photo! By the 1860s it only took 15 minutes.

When cameras were first invented, they could only take black and white photos. If people wanted colour photos, they had to paint them by hand.

Until the 1950s and 60s most shops were owned and run by one family. This photo was taken in about 1880. The shop in the photo is a **grocery shop**. What did it sell?

Money
Until 1971 British money was pounds, shillings and pence. There were 12 pence (12D or 12d) in 1 shilling (1s or 1/-) and 20 shillings in 1 pound (£1). All the prices in the pictures show this 'old money'.

The people in this photo are shopping in an open-air **market**. It was often cheaper to buy things at a market.

A boy is selling ice cream from a cart to other boys.

People carry their shopping in baskets. Carrier bags had not been invented.

The food was weighed on scales like these.

Can you find

- a brother and sister going shopping?
- two lots of cauliflower for sale?
- a market stall on wheels?

Norwich shopping arcade, around 1900

The shops in this shopping **arcade** were covered over. People stayed dry as they went from one shop to another.

People could buy fruit and flowers from this shop.

This shop sold watches. It also sold chains for the watches.

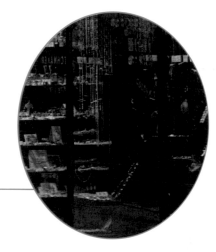

The chain fixed the watch to a man's waistcoat. The watch went in a pocket.

Can you find

- an empty vase?
- two heart-shaped photo frames?
- how the arcade was lit up when it got dark?

Bates' butcher's shop, 1900

Most shops in 1900 sold just one kind of thing. The shop in the photo is a butcher's shop. It sold meat.

This is a special display of meat for New Year.

The meat has labels saying where it came from.

The meat was **delivered** free to **customers'** houses. This boy did the deliveries.

Can you find
- Farmer Bates the butcher?
- a sign that says 'God Bless our Home'?
- meat from Lord Cadogan's land?

Villages did not have as many shops as towns did in 1901. **Shopkeepers** often did more than one job.

This shows the shopkeeper is a **chemist**. The board says he also sells medicine for animals, seeds, railway tickets and **insurance**!

The sign painted on the door (partly covered up) says the chemist takes out teeth, too. It says 'Teeth carefully extracted'.

Can you find

- the name of the shopkeeper?
- a sign that shows he sells cocoa?
- a **delivery** boy in his white apron?

An ironmonger's shop, 1933

Ironmongers sell things to use in the house and garden. This shop sold anything from a kettle to a cooker.

The shop sold electric light bulbs and shades.

Ranges like this one burned coal to cook food and heat water.

You put the washing in this machine and turned a handle to move it around.

Can you find

- the metal flour bins?
- two bathroom mirrors?
- the kettles?

A grocery shop in the 1940s

In this shop, the **customer** is telling the **shopkeeper** what she wants to buy. He fetches the things she wants.

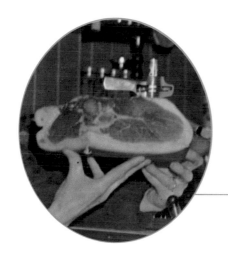

The shopkeeper cut slices of bacon on the machine next to him.

This shop sold flour in tins, not bags.

Biscuits came in big tins. The shopkeeper weighed them out for each customer.

Can you find

- some tins of soup?
- some tins of fish?
- how much a big bar of soap cost?

A supermarket in the 1950s

Supermarkets were new in the 1950s. People could do all their food shopping in one place. They collected the things they wanted in a basket or a trolley.

The signs in the shop told **customers** where to find the things they wanted.

People still cut all the bacon, cheese and meat for customers.

The people working here wore coats. The coats helped customers to find them.

Can you find

- the price of a large tin of Bartlett pears?
- where to find the flour?
- a woman stacking the shelves?

Supermarkets did not replace all family **grocery shops**. This shop was in Oxford.

The **shopkeeper** is weighing cheese for the **customer**.

The shopkeeper had to add up the prices in his head or on a piece of paper.

Biscuits still came in big tins for customers to buy just as many as they wanted.

What's different?

Look at the photos on pages 5, 18, 20. What's different? Think about:

- what the workers are wearing
- what the food is packed in.

Did you find?

Salisbury Market, 1895,
pages 6–7

Norwich shopping
arcade, around 1900,
pages 8–9

Bates' butcher's
shop, 1900,
pages 10–11

Carnforth village,
main street, 1901,
pages 12–13

An ironmonger's
shop, 1933,
pages 14–15

A grocery shop in the 1940s,
pages 16–17

A supermarket in
the 1950s,
pages 18–19

Glossary (What words mean)

arcade a covered place full of shops

chemist a person who sells medicines

customer a person who comes to a shop to buy something

deliver/delivery take or send the things a customer buys to their house

grocery shop a shop that sells food that you need for cooking (like flour and rice) as well as biscuits, tea, coffee and tinned food. Most grocers do not sell raw meat or vegetables.

insurance some people pay money every few weeks to an insurance company, so that they will get some money if things go wrong. If they insure their house or the things they own, the insurance company will give them money to help them replace anything that is lost, stolen or destroyed in a storm or fire.

market a place where food and other things are sold from stalls. Most markets are out in the open and some are only held once a week.

shopkeeper a person who owns or runs a shop

Index